Beady Eyed Women's Guide To Exquisite Beadwork:
An Off-Loom
Bead Weaving Primer

by Jeannette Cook & Vicki Star
© 1996

ISBN Number 1-889789-06-2

Cover Photo by
Jeff Tippett

Second Printing - September 1996

Written and Illustrated on a Macintosh Performa Computer

Published by: Beady Eyed Women, Enterprises
P.O. Box 60691
San Diego, CA 92166

Table of Contents

Pictured on the front cover is the **"Wild Haired, Level Headed Woman"** by *Jeannette Cook*. This piece uses all of the techniques in this book!

On the back cover, clockwise from top left, are:

Necklace - Square stitch (page 12) *JC*

Hatpin - Tubular Ndebele (page 5) *VS*

Bead Slug! - Right Angle Weave (page 6) *VS*

Bracelet - Combination of all techniques *VS*

Necklace - Combination of techniques *JC*

Evening Purse - Right Angle Weave (page 6) *VS*

Squash Blossom Earrings - Brick Stitch (page 18) *VS*

VS = created by *Vicki Star*   *JC* = created by *Jeannette Cook*

Welcome, Beady Eyed Friends!

We've been having so much fun learning new stitches, and experimenting with them! We encourage you to play and try different things, too. These instructions are just a starting point. Try a stitch with a different bead. See what would happen if you started to do peyote stitch off the edge of Right Angle Weave. Create "Sculptural" Ndebele Weave. What can you think of?

We believe that there are many right ways to do beadwork. These are the methods that we use, whether we learned them from a book, or a fellow Beady Eyed Woman, or through figuring it out on our own.

Check the back of this book for a listing of our Favorite Beading Books. There are some great books and wonderful classes and terrific people out there in the world! We would like to take this time to say a giant "Thank you!" and give a big hug to all the creative people who willingly share their knowledge.

One Bead at a Time...

Jeannette Cook

Vicki Star

Basics

General Directions

In general, start with 2 or 3 yards of thread, single or doubled as you prefer. Use a comfortable length of thread. The last thing you want when learning a new technique is to fight tangles from too long a thread. Thread your needle and wax your thread. (Remember to pull the <u>thread</u>, not the needle, across the wax.)

Vicki likes to use keeper beads, like this: Tie a keeper bead loosely about 6 inches from the tail end of the thread. This bead serves to keep the other beads from falling off the end of the thread as you begin work, and will be removed. Be sure that you leave enough tail to thread into a needle and tie off.

Jeannette likes to tie knots, like so: Tie a knot at the very end of your thread. Leave some space between the knot and your beads. Bead your first and second (and sometimes third) rows. When you get back to the knot end of your thread, tie the 2 ends together in a square knot, dab a little glue on the knot, and cut off the tail thread.

Refer to the *Beady Eyed Women's Guide to Exquisite Beadwork: A Peyote Stitch Primer* for Vicki and Jeannette's complete "thread theories".

As with any technique, the first row or two are the most important, as they set you up for the rest of the beadwork. Be patient with yourself, take your time. When I am learning a new technique, I sometimes start over 2 or 3 times until I know I've got it right. I have a drawer full of "False Starts" that I keep for repair beads and for inspiration. Who knows, that "mistake" may be perfect for something else, or the beginnings of a whole new technique.

Something I've noticed in my classes is that most beginning beaders try to keep their beadwork on the table. It is much, much easier to hold the work in your hand as you bead. Use the tail as a handle to help you get started. I wrap the tail of thread around my little finger (not too tightly, please) to help keep proper tension on the first couple of rows.

*Tip - If you are having problems learning the technique, get some inexpensive E beads (6°s), and try the stitch with these. It's easier to figure it out if you can really see what the beads are doing.

*Tip - I usually don't count the beginning row of beads any more. Just string on more than enough, and remove the extras when you take off the keeper bead.

Basics   (Cont.)

Changing Threads

Unless you are doing a smallish piece of beadwork, there will probably come a time when you will want to add more thread. Pay attention to which bead the thread is coming out of, as well as the direction of the thread. In most cases, you will want the new thread to be the same. Some people like to tie on a <u>new</u> thread <u>before</u> tieing off the <u>old</u> one, for just this reason.

If you are doing a snug technique, like peyote or brick stitch, you usually don't need to tie any knots. Just weave the thread in a zig-zag through the beadwork.

For more open stitches, we like to tie three knots with each thread for security. Follow the thread path through your beadwork and tie each knot around a thread in the beadwork like this:

Put your needle under the thread right where the needle comes out. Pull it up until there is a little loop of thread.

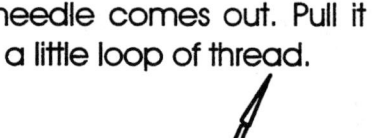

Put your needle through the loop.

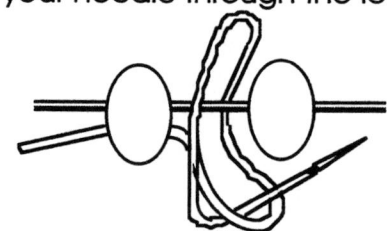

When you pull the thread tight, the knot will disappear inside a bead. Sew through a few more beads and tie another knot. Go through a few more beads and tie one more knot. Go through 1 or 2 more beads, and snip the thread as close to the beadwork as possible. You can melt any fuzzies with a lighter.

If thread is showing on top of a bead, something is wrong. Carefully pull out the thread and try again. Remember, <u>Technique Counts!</u> You wouldn't want that terrific pattern spoiled by a big, ugly knot right in the middle.

Plan ahead and tie off threads in a different area each time. This way you won't have to work around other knots or "stuffed" beads.

Also, be careful of the tension as you tie the knots and pull them tight. If you pull too tight, or have too many knots in the same place, you will get wrinkles in your beadwork. (Hey! Is this a good way to "gather" your beadwork? Remember, something might be "wrong" one time, but just what you intended the next!)

Ndebele Weave

Ndebele Weave is named for the Ndebele (pronounced en·de'·be'·le) Tribe in Africa. The beadwork gives the appearance of herringbone woven fabric. This stitch has more body than most. The beadwork folds well vertically, but curves, rather than folds, on the horizontal.

Flat Ndebele

The first group of beads on your thread will become the first two rows of the beadwork. The next row is actually the third. For clarity, we'll use 2 colors of beads. Once you understand the technique, you can graph patterns, and create designs!

Begin with a multiple of 4 beads. Let's use 16 for this sample. This will result in 4 "columns" of herringbone.

Tie a keeper bead on to the end of your thread, leaving a 6 inch tail, then string 16 light-colored beads. Leave a little room between the working beads and the keeper bead.

Add 1 dark-colored bead. (This bead is the first bead of the third row.) Skip the added bead and sew through the light bead (#16) closest to the needle, towards the tail. Skip two beads, (#15 & #14) sew through bead #13.

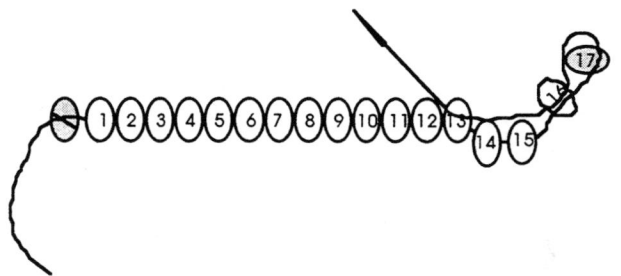

Add 2 dark beads, sew through the next bead (#12). Skip 2 light beads, sew through the third light bead (#9).

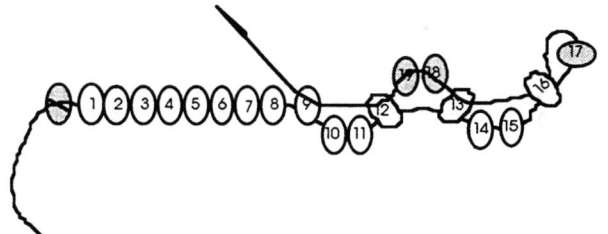

Ndebele Weave (Cont.)

*Add 2 dark beads, through the next light bead. Skip 2 light beads, through the next one. Repeat (from the *) across. Notice you are adding dark beads and going through light beads in this row.

Now, go across the row, adding 2 light beads and going down through 1 dark bead, then up through the next dark bead (added on the previous row) all the way across.

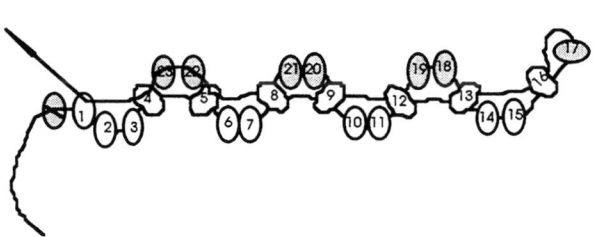

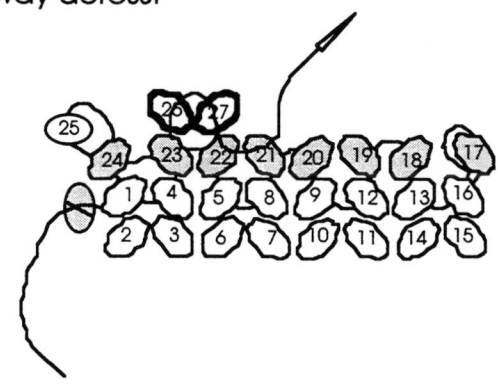

*Tip - Don't worry too much about how the beads lay, the next row pulls them into place.

When you get to the end of the row, add 2 beads (1 dark, 1 light). (You are adding the last bead of the current row and the first bead of the next row!)

Turn around, skip the light bead, sew through the dark bead that you just added. To snuggle the beads up tight, hold the dark bead between your thumb and finger, and pull on the thread. Bring your needle through the first bead of the next 2 bead set.

Keep on beading, always adding 2 beads, and going through 2 beads, until the piece is as tall as you want it to be. To finish the piece, add 1 bead of the current row color, and tie off your thread.

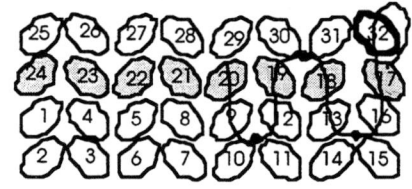

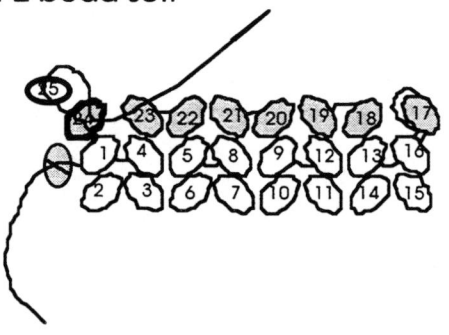

Ndebele Weave (Cont.)

Tubular Ndebele

Start with a multiple of 4 beads. (Remember the keeper bead.) Connect these into a circle by going through the first 2 beads. *Add two beads, sew through the next bead on the ring, skip 2 beads, through the next bead on the ring. Repeat from the *, all the way around.

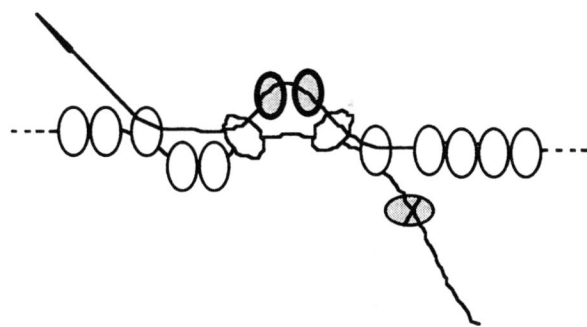

The "Step Up" - To finish the row, go up through the first bead of the second row and the first bead of the third row. (Remember, that first circle of beads is really the first two rows!)

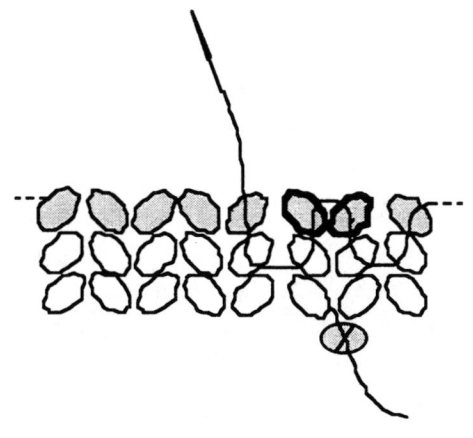

Add two beads, sew down through 1, up through 1, and so on, until the tube is as long as you like. Remember to "step up" to finish each row and begin the next.

*Tip - A nice way to finish the top and bottom edges is to add a bead between every other bead all the way across. This straightens the edges and makes them lay flat. It also provides a great foundation row for netting or other stitches.

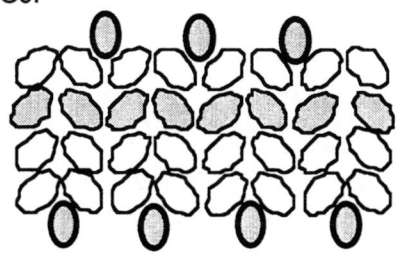

Right Angle Weave

David Chatt has recently popularized this technique, and creates fabulous vessels and flowers with Right Angle Weave. The beads sit at right angles to each other. (Gee, I wonder where the name came from...)

Single Needle, Right Angle Weave is a lot easier to do than to explain. Study the drawings, and look for the rhythm. Eventually, you can create wonderful patterns, but I recommend starting out with one color for the first row, then changing to a new color for the next row. Alternating colors for each row can help you to see where you are going.

This stitch can be done in one bead units for a tightly woven fabric, or several bead units for an open lattice.

*Definition - A **Unit** is a group of beads treated as one bead.

*Tip - No thread should show across "intersections".

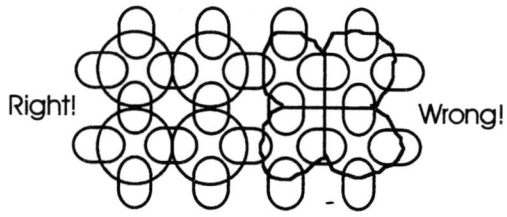

Right!   Wrong!

Right Angle Weave - Fabric

Traditional Base Row: String 4 beads in a circle. Hold the beads so the needle and thread are coming up, out of the right side bead.

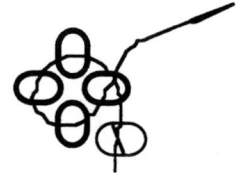

Add 3 beads. Sew in a circle up through bead #1, then continue on around the circle through 2 more beads in a clockwise direction.

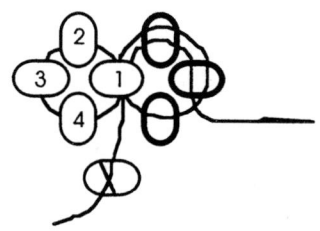

Add 3 beads. Sew in a circle down through the horizontal bead, then continue on around the circle through 2 more beads, in a COUNTERclockwise direction.

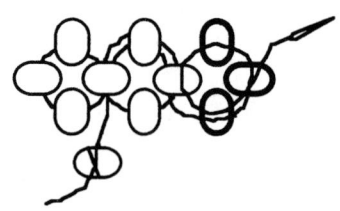

Continue adding 3 beads at a time in this manner, alternating directions with each circle, until the beadwork is the desired width.

Right Angle Weave (Cont.)

Turns and Additional Rows

Depending on how many beads wide your piece is, there are two methods of turning.

Turn A - At the end of the row, go through 1 more bead to set up the turn. Your needle should be coming out the last top bead. Let's call her the "turn" bead. If your needle is pointing in towards the middle of your beadwork, use turn A.

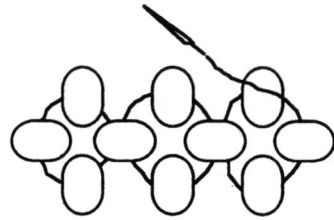

Add 3 beads. sew through the turn bead, and the next bead on new row (the first of the 3 added beads). (Your needle should be coming UP out of the beadwork.)

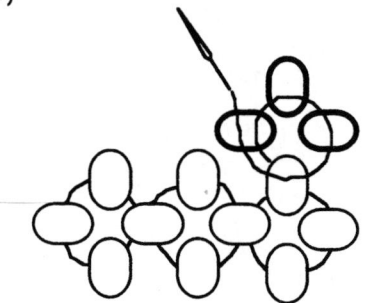

Step 1 - Turn the piece over, and add 2 beads. Go through 2 beads (clockwise) to make a circle. Notice the thread is again coming up out of the beadwork.

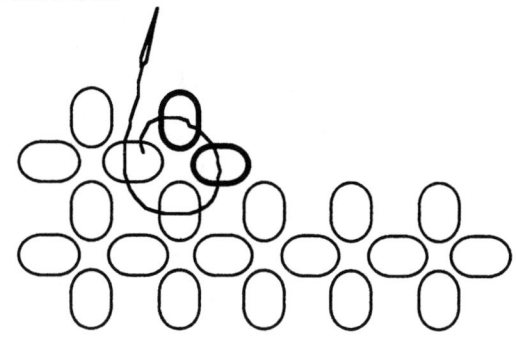

Thus, you must sew through 3 more beads to prepare for next circle.

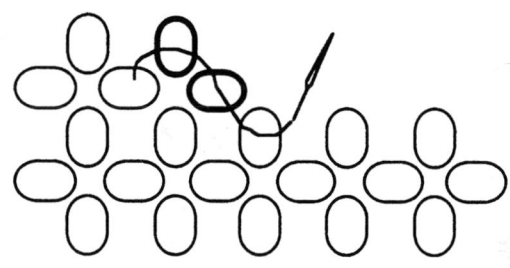

Step 2 - Add 2 beads, and go through 2 beads to make a circle (counterclockwise). Notice your thread is coming from down in the beadwork.

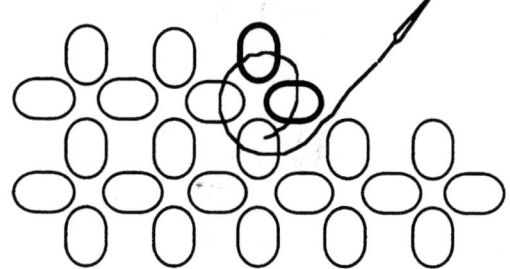

Right Angle Weave (Cont.)

Thus you must go up through 1 more bead to prepare for the next circle.

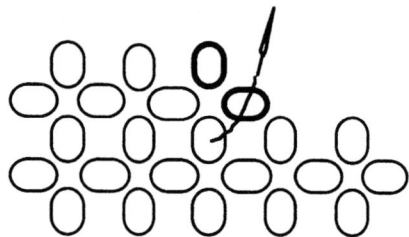

Continue across the row, alternating steps 1 and 2.

Turn B -Sew around through the last top bead (the "turn" bead). Use this B turn when your needle is pointing out, away from the beadwork.

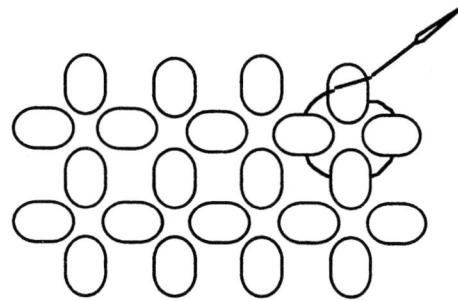

Add 3 beads. Sew through the turn bead (counter-clockwise), through the 3 added beads again, and 1 more bead to set up the next circle.

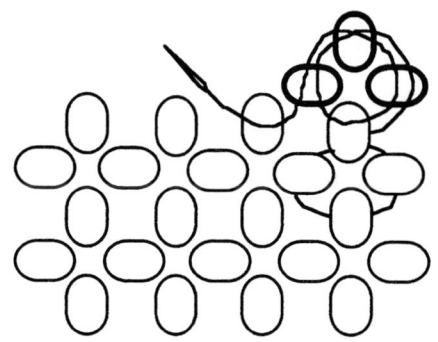

Turn your piece over. The next circle will be worked in a counterclockwise direction. In other words, when you do Turn B, do step 2 first, then step 1.

*Tip - To decrease to a point, simply turn one unit before the edge each time.

Right Angle Weave (Cont.)

Shortcut base row: String the desired number of beads. (Use an even number.) Go through the fourth bead from the needle in a circle.

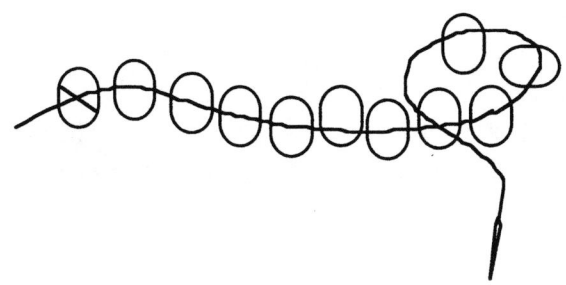

*Add 1 bead. Go through the second bead <u>away</u> from the tail.

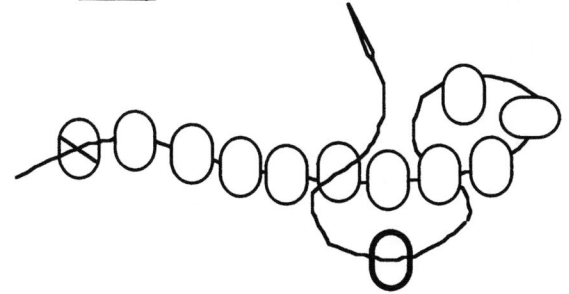

Pull both threads and adjust the square of beads. Repeat from * to end of row.

Right Angle Spiral
Start with a 4 bead circle.

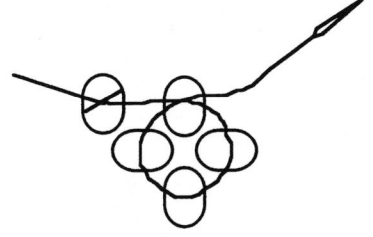

Add 3 beads and go through the same bead again, in the same direction. Go through one more bead.

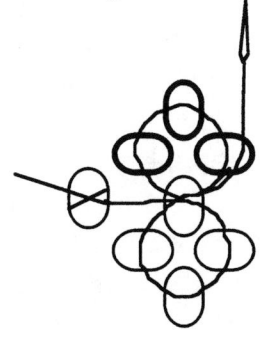

*Add three beads. Make a circle by sewing through the bead you came out of and 3 more beads.

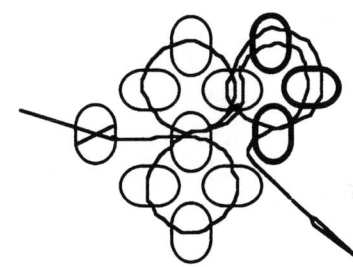

Add 3 beads and go through the one you came out of and one more bead.

Repeat from the *, always adding 3 beads, making a circle, then alternating between going through 1 more and 3 more beads.

Thread tension is important. Pull your thread tight when doing this stitch!

*Tip - You can add peyote, netting, or more right angle weave along the edge for a wider spiral!

Right Angle Weave (Cont.)

Lattice Style Right Angle Weave

The technique is the same as Right Angle Weave fabric. The only difference is, you may use any multiple of 4 beads for each circle. The thread path will pull the circle of beads into a square with the multiple number of beads on each side. For example, 12 beads will create a lattice with 3 beads on a side; 8 bead circles will have 2 beads on a side. We'll use 12 beads for this example.

Base row - String 12 beads. Make a circle by sewing through the first 3 beads.

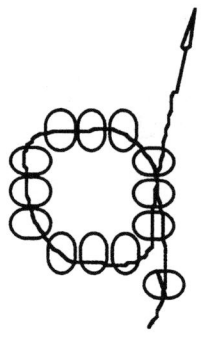

Add 9 beads, sew through 3 beads on the first circle, and 6 beads on the new circle (clockwise)

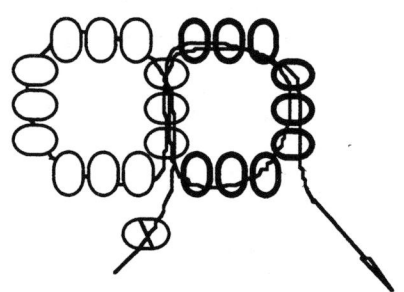

Continue - adding 9 beads, connecting through 3 beads, and sewing through 6 beads, alternating between clockwise and counterclockwise circles. (They should soon begin to look like squares.)

Refer to the previous section for directions on turning and additional rows. (Simply substitute 3 beads for every 1 in those instructions.)

*Tip - Add the same multiple of beads for each circle to get a flat piece of bead fabric. Or, experiment with different multiples and bead sizes for "Sculptural Right Angle Weave"!

*Tip - You can sew crystals or e-beads, etc. into the open latticework for a different look. Be careful not to pull the beadwork out of shape. The added bead must just fill the space.

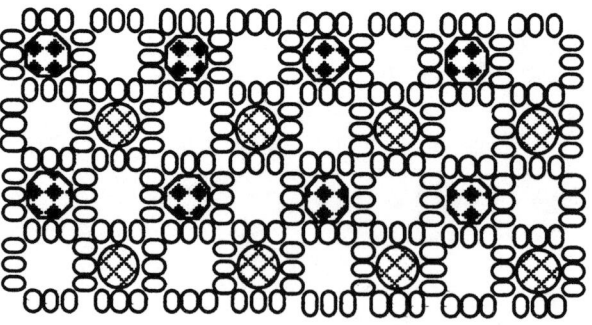

Right Angle Weave (Cont.)

Tubular Right Angle Weave

Surprise! This stitch can also be done in a tube!

Depending on the number of circles in the base row, your needle may be going in a different direction. Try turning the book or your beadwork over until the drawing matches what you are doing.

When the base row is long enough, add a unit of beads and sew through the other end.

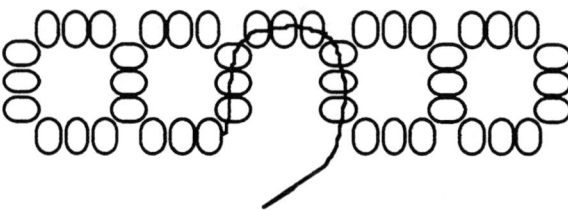

Add another unit, and sew on around the circle.

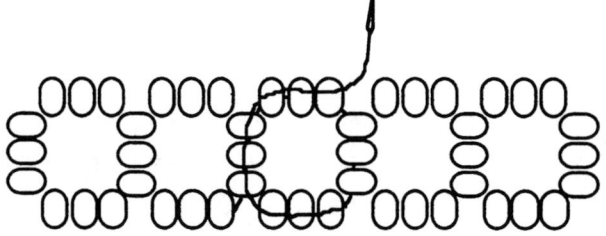

Add 3 units of beads and make a circle in the normal manner.

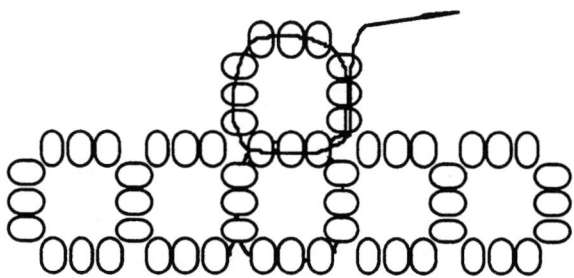

Continue beading around the tube. When you get to the end of the row, you will only have to add 1 unit (instead of 2) to connect the ends.

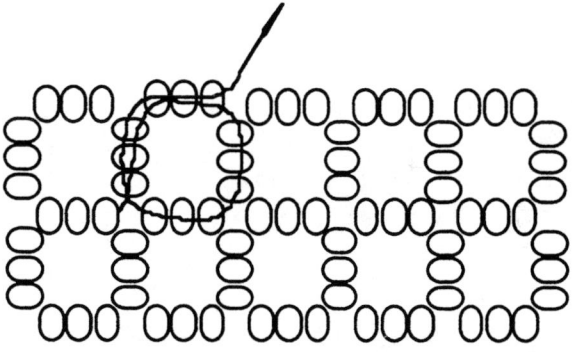

Run the thread around the connecting circle so no thread shows across the "intersections". Your thread path will always be in a circle. If you find yourself sewing straight along more than one circle of beads, make sure that you <u>meant</u> to do that!

*Tip - These drawings show units of three, but you can use any "Unit Count" you like.

Square Stitch

This stitch looks just like loomwork, only you don't need a loom, and you don't have to deal with all those warp threads! You can use cross-stitch or any square gridded pattern for design ideas.

Typically, this stitch is worked with an even number of beads. I have also noticed that most of the work done in square stitch is done with beads that are all the same size. Well, Vicki and I got bored with that pretty quickly and worked out how to use different sizes and shapes of beads together. Along with that, we found it necessary to work with odd and even numbers together.

Basic Square Stitch

We will begin with an even number of beads, but use several of each type together in your first row.

Needle back around and through the third and fourth beads folding the first and second beads over as shown below.

Now needle back through the 2 "folded" beads, coming out in the direction of the line of beads in your original strand. (The dotted lines show direction of the thread inside the beads.)

Add two more beads, and go back through, around and out again.

Continue adding beads two at a time until you have two rows.

Start the third row by adding 2 more beads, fold them over and needle through the above two beads and the beads you just added.

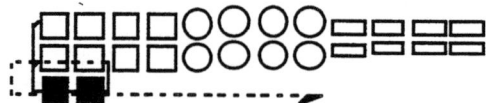

When you get to the end of the row, flip your piece over. Add more rows the same way.

Square Stitch (Cont.)

Once you are comfortable enough with the technique, play with the <u>quantities</u> in the same row. Here I show adding three beads at a time. These beads are all the same size. You can mix bead <u>sizes</u> in each increment as well.

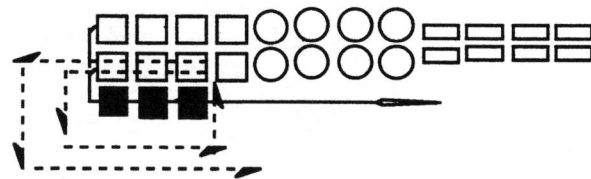

Decreasing

Make steps by turning and square stitching back toward the beginning of the row before you reach the end. Then thicken the new section by square stitching back and forth in the shortened area. Repeat this step a few more times until the piece looks like stair steps.

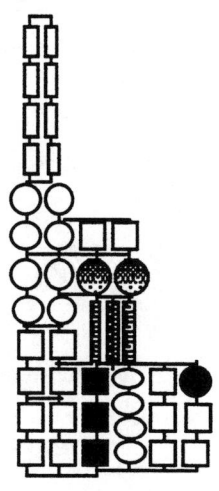

Increasing

To make your beadwork wider or longer, string some beads out past the last row of the original beadwork. (They can be even or odd, all the same size, or varied sizes). I am using all the same size and an even number for this example.

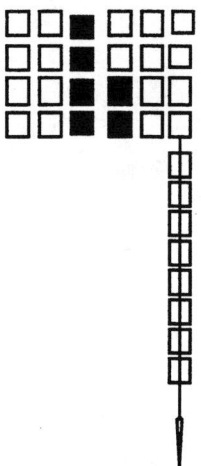

Add two more beads and sew back through the two above them, then through the added two beads. Your thread will be headed up toward the main body of your work. The new beads are now folded over.

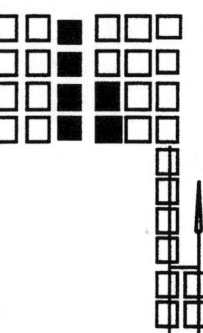

13

Square Stitch (Cont.)

Add two more beads and needle down through the beads at their sides, then back up through the two new beads. Repeat this step until the second row begins to extend along the main piece of beadwork.

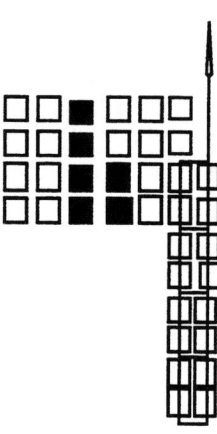

Hiding Edge Threads

To add a row of beads across the top (or thread) edge, stitch a strand of beads across from one end bead to the opposite end bead.

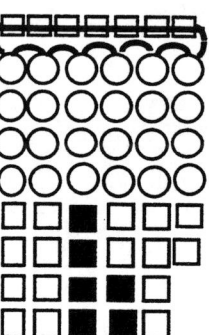

Keep adding rows along the entire side until the beadwork is wide enough to suit your taste. You can increase anywhere in the beadwork. Just be sure you connect to the original piece so your work won't be floppy.

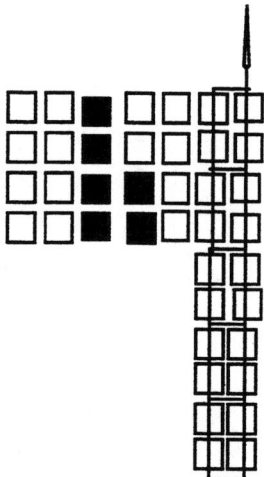

Square Stitch (Cont.)

Now tack the new strand of beads down to the thread loops in the edge of the beadwork.

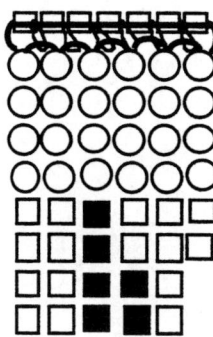

Continue the square stitch along this edge. You have now changed the direction of the stitches. This adds a nice texture to the look of your work.

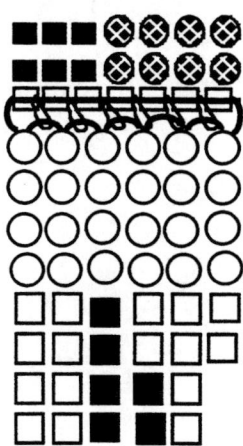

Extensions

Bring your needle out the side of your beaded piece between two beads. (Use the side where no holes show).

String an even number of beads. Sew back through the last four, letting the two end beads fold over. Now back up through the two folded over beads so that your needle is headed back up toward the main piece.

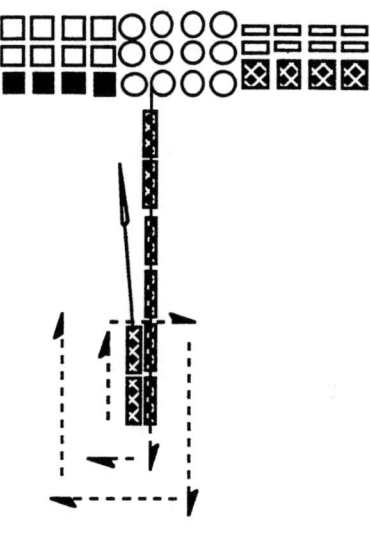

Square Stitch (Cont.)

Continue square stitching rows of beads, tacking each row to the main part of the beadwork. Soon you will be ready to add another extension. Look for a good place to do so and bring your thread out at that point.

Keep adding beads using the square stitch technique. Improvise for filling in areas where the beads don't connect perfectly. You can stitch a bead or two just about anywhere to fill in gaps while you are beading!

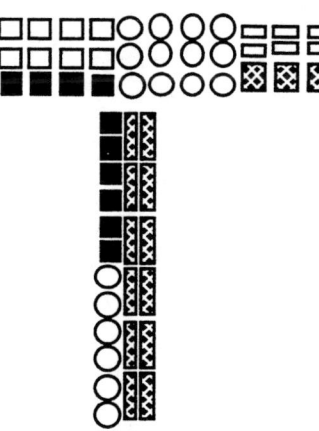

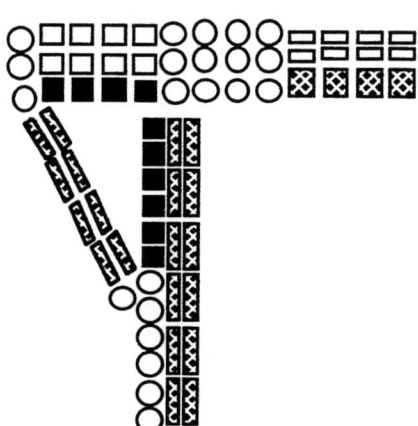

Square Stitching - Diagonally

To create a line of beads diagonally, string your strand between two points in your piece. Attach the thread wherever seems logical. (Connect through a bead, or around the threads between beads, in the main body of your piece.)

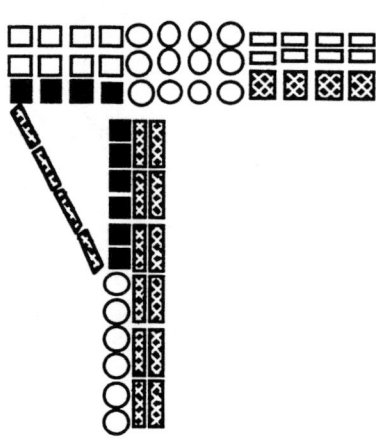

Square Stitch (Cont.)

Large Beads

Adding large beads in combination with small beads is just as easy as adding any other beads. Add a seed bead or two, then the large bead and some more small beads, enough to connect the two square stitched areas. Now square stitch back and forth along the small connecting beads until the beadwork extends past the large bead. You may now string more beads from that section to another area.

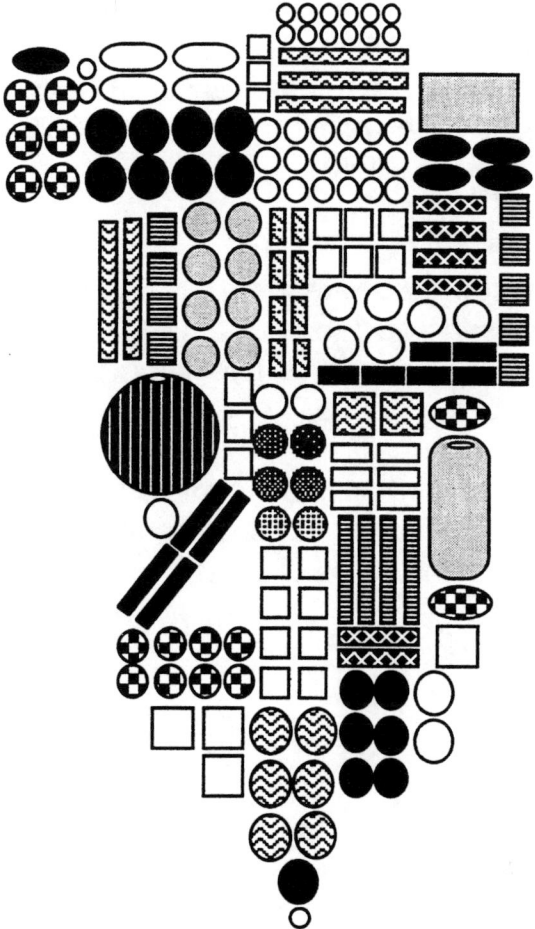

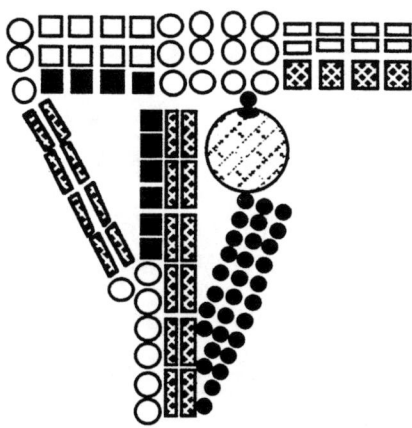

Continue branching out in different directions and experimenting with size variations until you have a piece large enough to wear. You can make earrings, a brooch, or even a necklace using this wonderful technique.

Brick Stitch

Although more commonly used for triangle-topped earrings, Nan C. Meinhart makes wonderful beaded baskets with brick stitch (also called Comanche Stitch).

Traditional Base Row

This is the traditional method. It makes a firmer base, with more thread in the holes of the beads.

String 2 beads. Make a circle by going through the first and second beads again, in the same direction.

Add 1 bead. Go down through the second and up through the third bead.

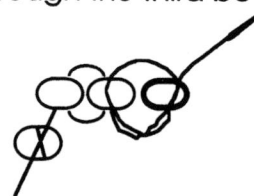

Continue adding single beads and sewing through them in a circle until the desired length is reached. (I like to use odd numbers for earrings as this will allow a center fringe and a balanced design.)

Alternate Base Row

I usually use this one. I like it because it's quicker and there are not as many threads in each bead, allowing room to add more fringe, etc.

String the desired number of beads. Leave some space between your beads and the keeper bead. Sew through the second from the last bead (in a circle). Pull on both the needle and the tail threads to make the beads sit evenly, side by side.

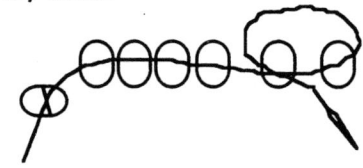

Now, go through the next bead, (sew away from the tail), and pull the threads.

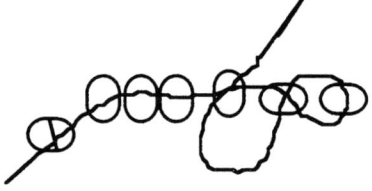

Continue to sew through each bead and tighten the threads until you reach the end of the row.

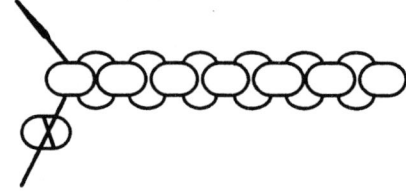

Brick Stitch   (Cont.)

Adding a Row

Depending on the method used, your needle will either be coming out the same bead as the tail (in the opposite direction), or it will be on the other end. It doesn't matter, just flip the base around so the needle is on the left, and continue.

Decreasing

Add two beads and catch (go under) the loop of thread between the second and third beads of the base row. Now go back up through the second bead of the two just added.

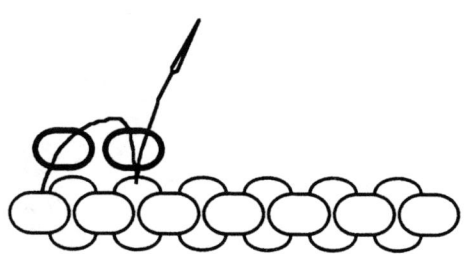

Add another bead, catch the thread between the next two beads, and go back up through the bead just added.

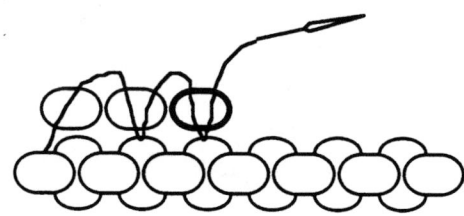

Continue on across the row. When you get to the end of the row, just flip the piece over, and keep going. Remember to add 2 beads at the beginning of each row.

As you can see, each row will be one bead shorter than the previous row. You'll end up with a triangle, stacked sort of like the milk bottles at a carnival booth.

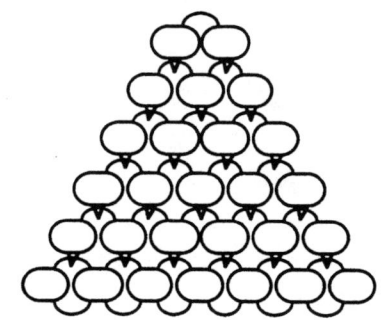

Brick Stitch (Cont.)

Increasing

If you want your piece to get wider. add two beads in the normal manner, but catch the thread between the <u>first</u> and <u>second</u> beads of the previous row.

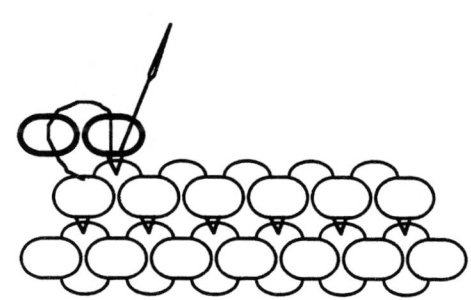

When you get to the end of the row, add one more bead, go down through the end bead of the previous row, catch the thread below it, and sew back up through both beads.

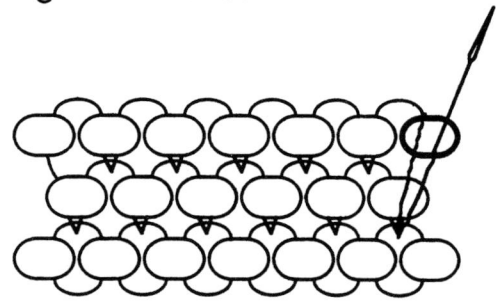

Shapes

To create shapes, (diamonds, etc.) start at the widest row and work up, then turn the beadwork over and work "down".

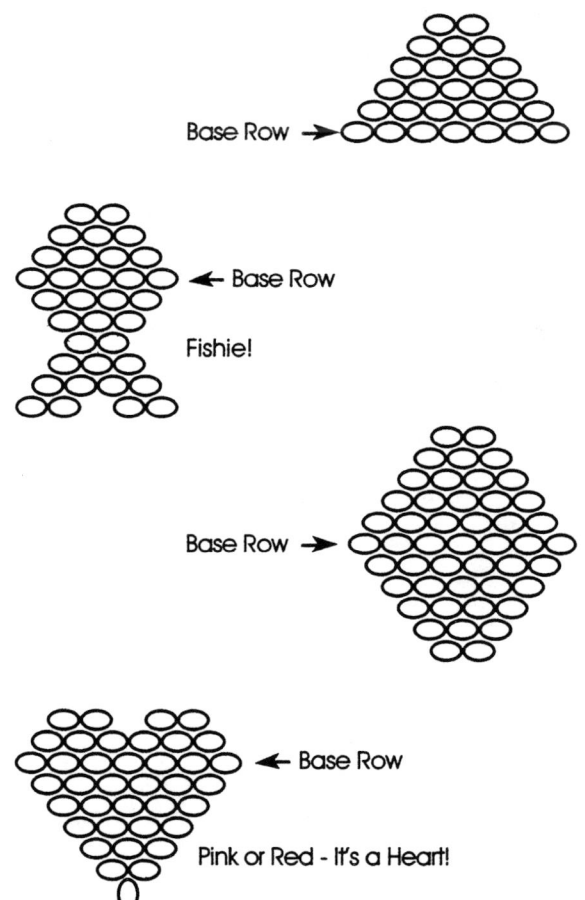

Base Row →

← Base Row

Fishie!

Base Row →

← Base Row

Pink or Red - It's a Heart!

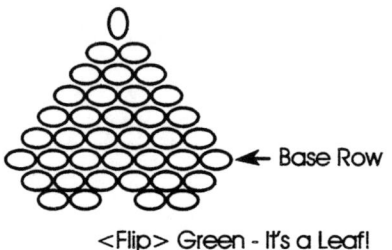

← Base Row

<Flip> Green - It's a Leaf!

Brick Stitch <u>(Cont.)</u>

If you want a "rectangle", alternate between increasing and decreasing rows.

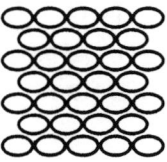

For a more abstract shape, stop two or more beads from the end of the row. You can also connect shapes to create stars, flowers, etc.

*Tip - Rows may be made with bugles or multiples of beads as one "unit".

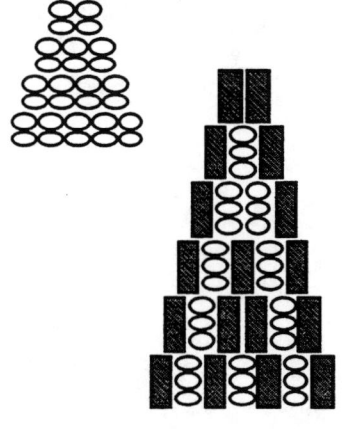

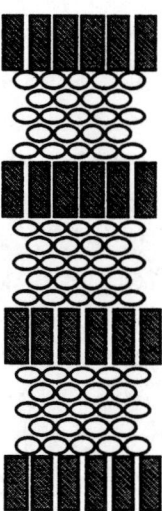

Peyote Stitch Variations

We have covered this stitch in other *Beady Eyed Women's Guides to Exquisite Beadwork,* but wanted to include a few more variations on this versatile technique.

Double Peyote Stitch

Put an even number of 2 beads "sets" on the threaded needle. Treat each set of two beads as a unit of one. Alternate colors if it helps to see a pattern.

Add 2 beads. Needle back through the second set from the beads you just added.

Add two beads, needle through the fourth set of two, etc.

When you reach the end of the row, both the tail and the needle threads should be coming out of the same set of beads. Tie your two threads together, put glue or nail polish on the knot. Cut the tail thread off. Add two beads and begin row four!

Double Peyote sets you up to make a transition to bugle beads or larger beads.

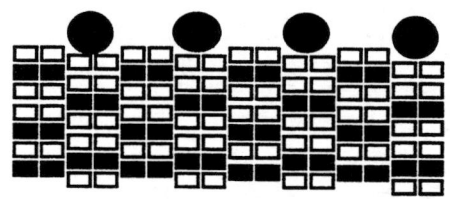

Peyote Stitch - Bugle Bead Style

I don't use the silver lined bugles any more because they tend to cut my thread so badly. Joyce Scott says to put a seed bead on either end of the bugle to protect the thread. I suggest you try it. (You can also keep a small file or piece of emery paper in your bead box. File the ends of sharp beads that you just have to use. Or, coat the ends with clear nail polish.) I have found the matte finished Japanese bugles to be much "safer" to use.

Peyote Variations (Cont.)

Simply treat the bugles as you would any other bead. Begin with an odd number of beads.

Needle back through the third bead, heading for the thread end.

Add a bead, go through the fifth bead and so on until you reach the end of the row. (Tie the two threads together, glue and cut the short thread.) Peyote stitch back and forth until you are ready to do something different.

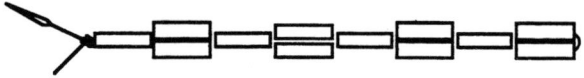

Experiment with different sizes and shapes of beads between the bugles. Make a transition from bugles to the other types of beads and continue peyote stitching. This is a fun way to get wonderful textures in your piece.

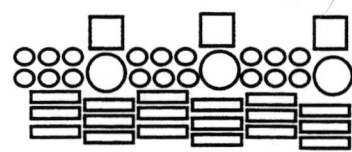

Square Holes

Once you have completed a few rows of peyote stitch using seed beads or delica beads, you can begin to create square holes.

Starting at the "down" bead end of your peyote stitch piece, *add a bead, go through an "up" bead, all the way across the tab. Now turn and peyote back to the edge. Repeat from the *. Keep peyote stitching back and forth. You decide how tall you want to make each little tab. I like to make them six to eight rows tall.

Now work back down to the main peyote piece and over three to six beads and make another tab.

23

Peyote Variations (Cont.)

Repeat this all the way across the main piece, if you like, or stop at three or four tabs.

To connect the tabs, work your thread out the top edge of the end tab that is facing the other tabs. *String enough beads to reach the top edge of the next tab. Work the needle over to the other side of this tab and repeat from the *. Continue until you have connected all the tabs.

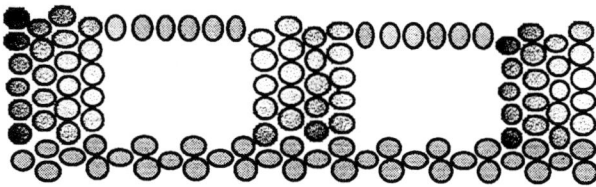

Peyote stitch along the top of the tabs and connectors until you feel you have enough rows.

Stair Steps - Increasing

At the end of a row, add three beads and go back through the first bead.

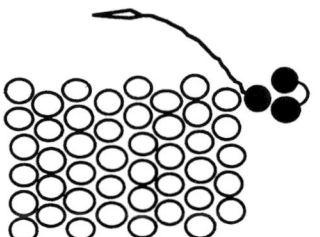

Add a bead and sew through the first "up" bead in the original peyote stitch area.

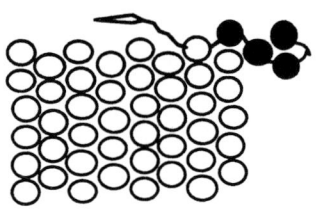

Continue peyote stitching to the end of the row and back. Stitch all the way to the end including the three new beads. Do about three to four rows of peyote stitch in the new color.

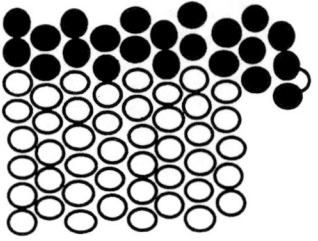

Peyote Variations (Cont.)

Begin a new stair step with the three beads. I like to change colors with each stair step.

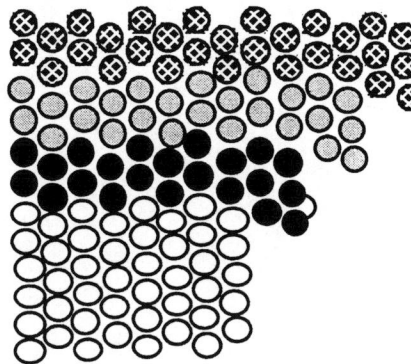

Stair Steps - Decreasing

*About three beads before the end of the row, turn and peyote stitch back to the opposite end.

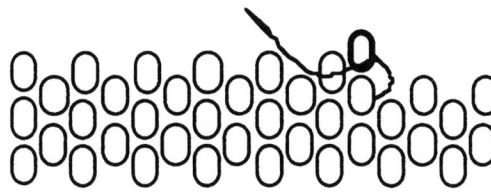

Turn, add a bead and peyote back to the shortened end. Repeat from the* for as many times as you like, then repeat the decreasing steps from the * again. Create as many stair steps as you wish!

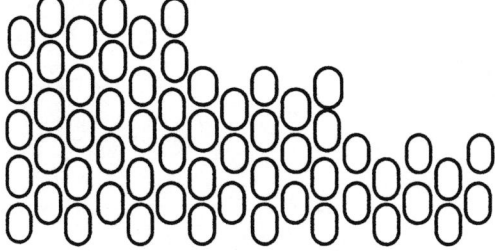

Decreasing at an Angle

When you reach the edge of your beadwork, sew through the loop between the two end beads. Pull the thread tight and go back through the "down" bead and the next "up" bead. Notice, no bead was added.

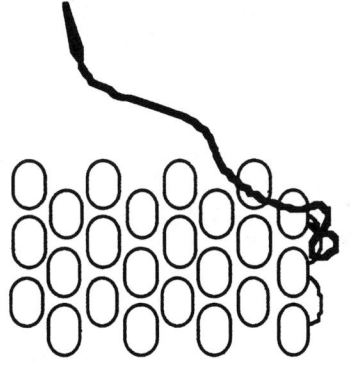

Now add a bead and continue peyote stitching back to the other edge.

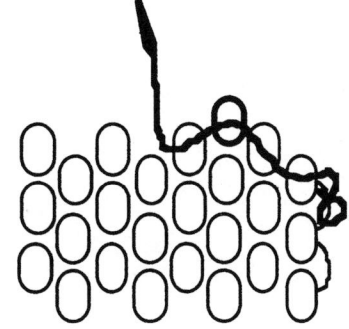

<u>Peyote Variations</u>   (Cont.)

*When you reach the decreased edge, don't add a bead, just loop your thread around the thread between the bead you are coming out of and the next bead down. Turn back and go through the "down" bead and the next "up" bead. Continue peyote stitching to the other edge and back.

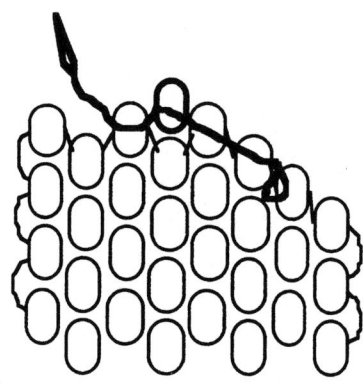

Repeat from the *, as many times as you like.

Connecting!

You can connect one stitch to the other in many ways. Sometimes it will be obvious, like doing brick stitch on the edge of peyote beadwork, and vice versa. Other times it will take a little ingenuity to connect the edges smoothly with no thread showing.

You can bead along, and change from one stitch to another.

You can connect two separate pieces by "zipping" them up with needle and thread. You can also add one or more beads between the 2 edges.

Try gathering the edges of one piece before attaching it to the next. Sew one piece on top of or at right angles to the other.

Connect 3 or more straight edges for a 3 dimensional form.

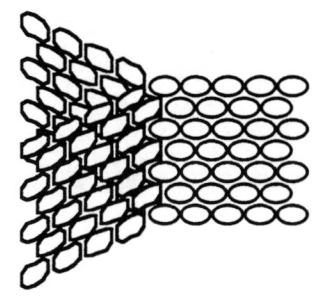

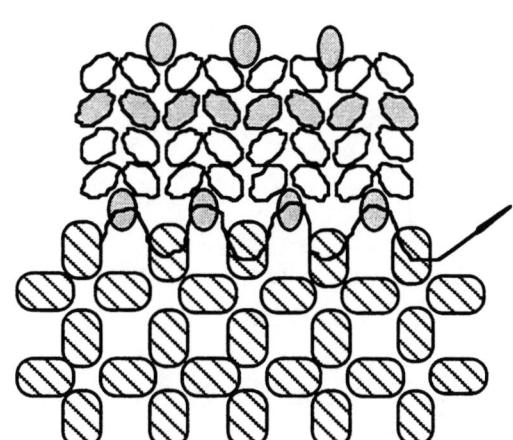

Our Favorite Bead Books

The following is a list of some of our favorite Bead Books. Ask for them at your local Bead Store.

Bead Work, Jules & Kaethe Kliot, Lacis Publications

Beaded Amulet Purses, Nicolette Stessin, Beadworld Publishing

Beadweaving (New Needle Techniques & Original Designs), Ann Benson, Sterling Publishing

Classic Earring Designs, Nola May, Eagle's View Publishing

Creative Beaded Earrings, Veon Schunzel, Veon Creations

Fearless Beadwork (Improvisational Peyote Stitch), Joyce J. Scott, Incognegro Unlimited

Flat Peyote Stitch, Michael White Owl, White Owl Publications

Indian Bead-Weaving Patterns, Horace Goodhue, Bead - Craft

Innovative Beaded Jewelry Techniques, Gineke Root, Lacis Publications

The New Beadwork, Kathlyn Moss and Alice Scherer, Harry N. Abrams, Inc.

Picot Lace (Innovative Beadwork), Sandy Forrington, Picot Press

Simply Beads, Betty J. Weber and Anne Duncan, Western Trimming Corp.

Speaking With Beads, Jean Morris and Eleanor Preston-Whyte, Thames and Hudson

Those Bad Bad Beads, Virginia L. Blakelock, Uni-Syn

And, of course, look for the other books in *The Beady Eyed Women's Guide* Series!

Bead Magazines

Bead & Button, Conterie Press

The Bead Bugle (Diskazine for Windows users), Williams & Assoc.

Jewelry Crafts, Miller Magazines, Inc.

Lapidary Journal, Lapidary Journal, Inc.

Ornament Magazine, Ornament, Inc.

Whispering Wind Magazine, Written Heritage (Native American Beadwork)

Peyote and Brick Stitch Graph

Turn the graph sideways for brick stitch!

Take these pages to your favorite copy store. Have them make you a transparency. Lay the transparency on top of the picture you want to chart, then make another copy. . . Viola! You have a charted graph!

You can also reduce or enlarge these graphs according to your bead size.

Peyote and Brick Stitch Graph

Right Angle Weave Graph

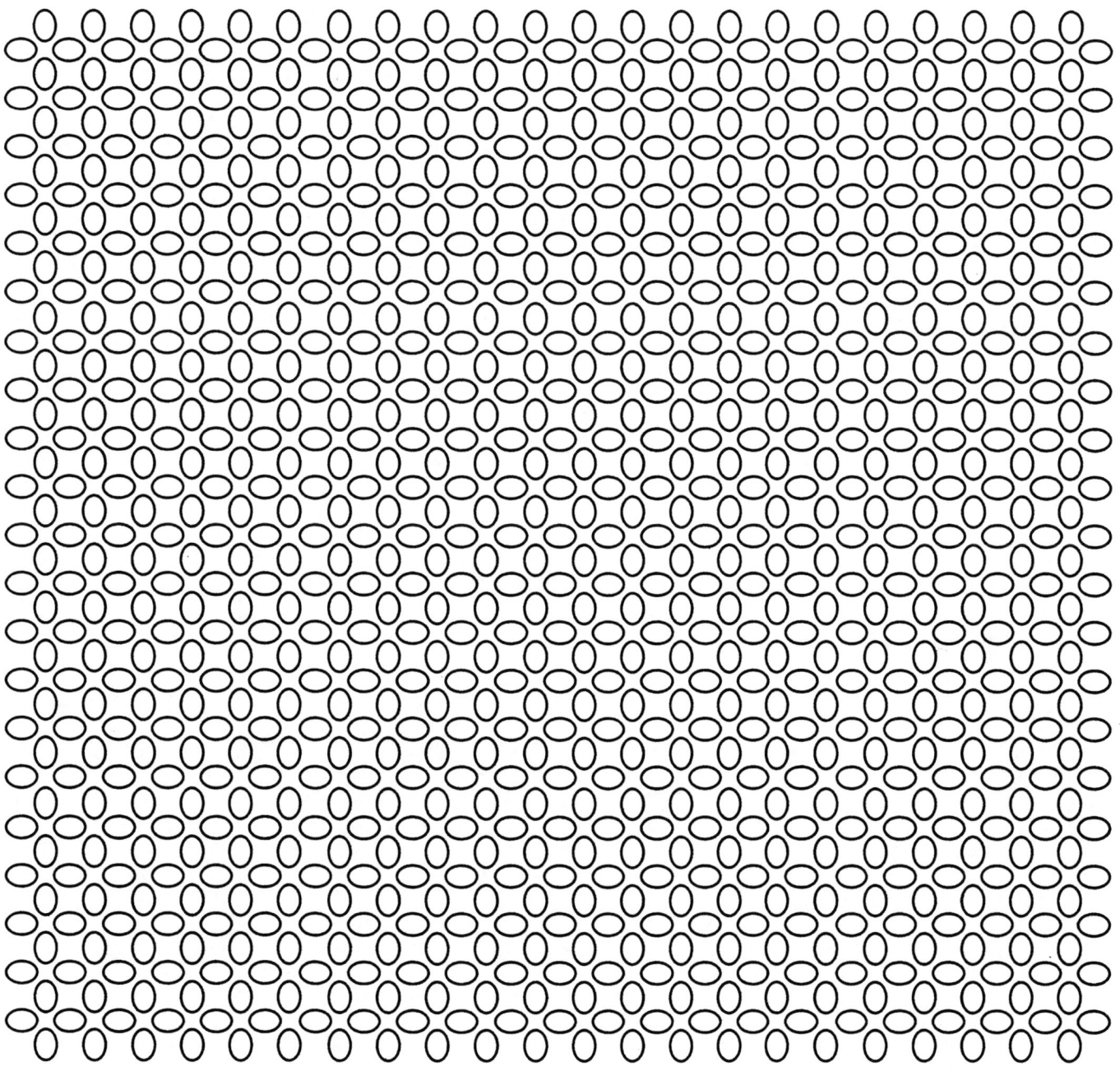

Right Angle Weave Graph

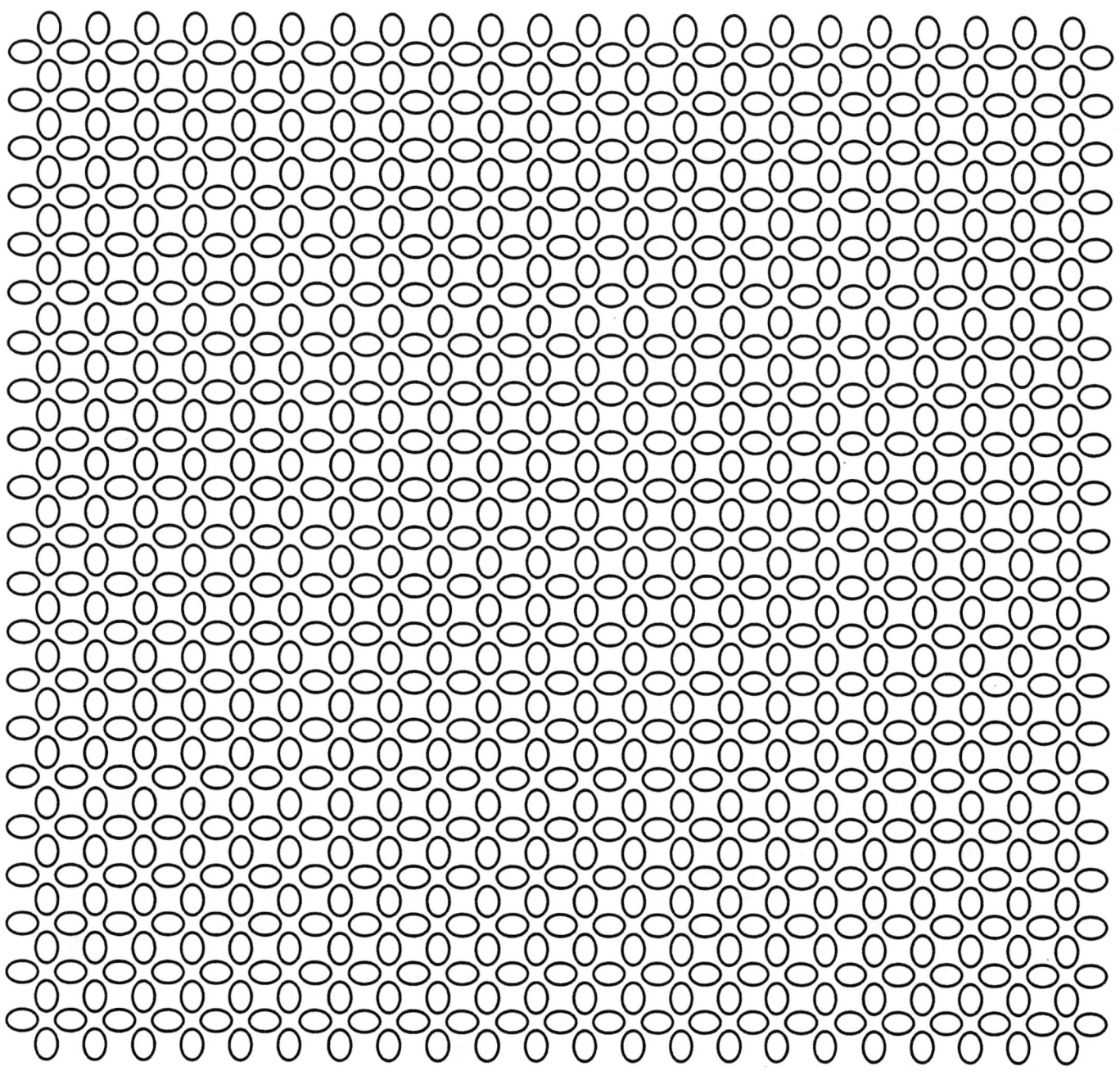

Ndebele Graph Paper

Ndebele Graph Paper

Square Stitch Graph

Square Stitch Graph